Meet the Cha

Mustafa and Arwa Adventure Series

ISBN-13: 978-1547156481
ISBN-10: 1547156481

MUSLIM PILLARS

This book belongs to:

_____

www.muslimpillars.com

Mustafa and Arwa go on a RAMADAN ADVENTURE

by Mekram Mohammad

Dedicated to my loving wife, Mai.

Mustafa and Arwa are excited for Ramadan to start.

Once you spot the Ramadan moon, a warm feeling enters the Muslim heart.

Mustafa and Arwa fast during the day and pray taraweeh at night.

That means no eating during the day, not even one bite!

When the night is dark and you can't hear a peep...

Muslims are calling to Allah while everyone else is asleep.

Suhur is the time for dua and pre-dawn meal.

Filling your tummy with food and blessings, now that's a pretty good deal!

Mustafa and Arwa use their time to do good and share.

Remembering to help people everywhere.

It doesn't matter if you have work or school.

Remembering Allah will give you all the energy and fuel.

The month of Ramadan is the time for forgiveness and sacrifice.

Make sure to ask Allah for the highest level of paradise!

Iftar is the post sunset meal to break your fast.

You made it through the whole day, it's time to eat at last!

The month of Ramadan will come and go.

It'll be Eid-el-fitr before you know!

Ramadan Glossary

- Fasting is the **fourth Pillar** of Islam

- Ramadan is the **ninth month** of the hijri Calendar

- Laylatul Qadr is the night of **power**

- Suhr - the meal consumed at **dawn** before the start of the fast

- Iftar - the **sunset** meal to ends the day's fast

- Dates - It is customary to break the fast with this sweet fruit, following the Sunnah (practice) of the Prophet Mohammed(pbuh). Dates are rich in several **vitamins and minerals**, which release a burst of energy when consumed.

The End!